AMAZING MATH MAGIC

OLIVER HO

Illustrated by Jeff Sinclair

Sterling Publishing Co., Inc.
New York

DEDICATION

This book is dedicated to my brother, Christopher.

Library of Congress Cataloging-in-Publication Data Available

10   9   8   7   6   5   4   3   2

First paperback edition published in 2002 by
Sterling Publishing Company, Inc.
387 Park Avenue South, New York, N.Y. 10016
© 2001 by Oliver Ho
Distributed in Canada by Sterling Publishing
c/o Canadian Manda Group, One Atlantic Avenue, Suite 105
Toronto, Ontario, Canada M6K 3E7
Distributed in Great Britain and Europe by Chris Lloyd at Orca
Book Services, Stanley House, Fleets Lane, Poole BH15 3AJ,
England.
Distributed in Australia by Capricorn Link (Australia) Pty. Ltd.
P.O. Box 704, Windsor, NSW 2756 Australia
Printed in China
All rights reserved

Sterling ISBN 0-8069-6017-5 Hardcover
               0-8069-7413-3 Paperback

CONTENTS

3. MAGIC WITH COINS 69

4. MAGIC WITH SHAPES 79

INDEX 96

INTRODUCTION

When you perform the tricks in this book, you'll have people believing you can read minds, calculate huge sums quicker than lightning, and make predictions that work every time! More importantly, you'll be able to entertain yourself, your friends, and your family with cool tricks anywhere, at any time.

Many of the tricks can be done with just a pen and paper, or a calculator. Some involve a deck of cards, some coins, or some dice. Other tricks use props that you can easily make by yourself, and others use items that you'll find at the dinner table.

All of the magic tricks in the book involve some principle of mathematics, either in their secret or in their presentation. They're all easy to learn and can be mastered with only a little bit of practice.

What You'll Need

At the beginning of each trick's description, you'll find a list of all the materials you'll need to perform it. Here's a complete list of everything you would need to perform every trick in this book:

- Paper and pens
- A calculator
- Two or more dice
- A deck of cards
- Index cards (or business cards)
- Twenty to thirty coins
- Strips of cloth or paper
- Scissors

- Paper money
- Paper clips
- Drinking glasses
- String
- Two forks

Patter and Performing

In the descriptions for some of the tricks in this book, you'll find suggested "patter"—things to say during the routine. Keep in mind that these are just suggestions. They're a good place to start, but it's always better and more fun to invent your own, more personalized routines and stories for these magic tricks.

You should always practice these tricks several times in front of a mirror or a good friend before you try them out on an audience.

I.
MAGIC WITH NUMBERS

ONE THOUSAND EIGHTY-NINE

The principle behind this trick is one of the most useful ones in mathematical magic. You can use it to perform many, many tricks. The key is that they have to involve the numbers 9, 18, or 1089.

🎩 The Effect

Before the trick begins, write down a prediction. Starting with a random three-digit number, the spectator makes a series of calculations and ends up with the "random" number 1089, which matches your prediction exactly. Then you can repeat the trick with predictions of 9 or 18.

☚ Materials
Paper
Pen
Calculator

☞Preparation

Write the number 1089 on a piece of paper, or on your arm (under your sleeve), or with your finger on a windowpane (so it'll show up when you use your breath to fog up the glass). Use your imagination to come up with a dramatic place to reveal your prediction.

The easiest way is simply to write the number down on a piece of paper in front of everyone before the trick begins—making sure no one can see exactly what you're writing. Then fold the paper and leave it in full view on the table.

The Routine and Patter

1. Give the spectator a piece of paper and a pen—and maybe a calculator. (For mathematical magic tricks it's very important that your spectators perform the arithmetic correctly.)

2. Ask the spectator to write down a three-digit number near the top of the paper. Say, "Just to make it interesting, make it have three different numbers." If you have an audience, you could also have three people each coming up with one digit for the three-digit number.

3. Say, "Let's add another random number, and we'll make it so random that we won't even have anyone choose it: Reverse your three-digit number. If this number is larger than the first, write it above that one. If it's smaller, write it below. Now subtract the smaller number from the larger number."

4. Ask if the answer has two or three digits. If it's two, then you know the answer is 99. (You can use this information later; see below.) Say, "We need to keep it at three digits to make it difficult. Write a zero in front of the number." If the answer already has three digits, everything's fine.

5. Say, "Reverse the digits in your answer and write that number below your answer. Now add these two three-digit numbers together."

6. The answer to this is always 1089. Be sure to reveal your prediction as dramatically as possible.

Here are some ways you can change your prediction (or repeat the trick):

• Predict 18. After the first subtraction (step 3), the sum of the numbers in the two- or three-digit answer is always 18.

• Predict 9. If the answer to the first subtraction (step 3) has three digits, the middle digit is always 9. Have the spectator drop the first and last digits. The result will match your prediction.

• Predict 9. If the answer to the first subtraction (step 3) has three digits, the total of the two end digits (the first and last digits) is always 9.

• Predict 99 (or 18, or 9). If the answer to the first subtraction (step 3) has two digits, it's always 99. You could total them to get 18, and then total those digits to get 9.

• Predict 18 (or 9). If you add up the digits in the final answer (1089), you'll get 18. Again, you can add up those digits to get 9.

For example:

The spectator writes down 432.

$$
\begin{array}{r}
432 \\
-234 \\
\hline
198 \\
\end{array}
$$
(Middle digit 9; $1 + 9 + 8 = 18$; $1 + 8 = 9$)

$$
\begin{array}{r}
198 \\
+891 \\
\hline
1089 \\
\end{array}
$$
($8 + 1 = 9$)

MATH TELEPATHY

🎩 The Effect

The spectator writes down a large number, performs some math with it, then circles one of the digits in the answer. You telepathically discover the circled number.

☞ Materials

Pen
Paper

☞ Preparation

Absolutely none! This trick works so well you don't even have to be there for it. You could even do it over the telephone!

The Routine and Patter

1. Ask the spectator to write down any number. It can be three, four, or five digits long.

I HAVE THREE DIGITS!... ON MY FOOT!

2. Tell them to mix up the digits of that number, and rearrange them in any order. For example, 123 could become 132, 213, or 231.

3. Ask them to subtract the smallest rearranged number from the largest rearranged number. (Get them to double check!)

4. Ask them to circle one of the digits in the answer. Say, "Don't circle a zero. That would make it too easy."

5. Say, "There's no way for me to know how many digits you have left in your answer, or what they are. Concentrate on the number that you circled. Now, in any order, I want you to slowly read off the numbers that you didn't circle."

6. Here's where your adding skills get a workout. If the spectator reads them too quickly, tell them to slow down and act like you're trying to read their mind. Add up all the numbers that the spectator tells you. If the final result has more than one digit, add those digits together. If that result has more than one digit, add the digits together again, and keep going until you end up with a single-digit answer.

7. Subtract this number from nine, and the result matches the circled number! Try it for yourself. It works every time.

8. Now, you could reveal the answer right away. Or you could build up the effect by telling them again how impossible it is for you to know the answer. They chose a large random number, which they used to come up with another random number, and all they did in the end was circle a number. Look at them with your best mind-reading face, and reveal the answer as dramatically as you can.

For example:

$$\begin{array}{r} 231 \\ -213 \\ \hline 18 \end{array}$$

If person circled 1, then $9 - 8 = 1$.
If person circled, 8, then $9 - 1 = 8$.

THE NINE MACHINE

This is a "human calculator" secret from a long time ago. It turns your fingers into an instant number 9 calculating machine.

Materials
Pen (optional)

Preparation

Hold your hands palms-down in front of you with your fingers straight out. Imagine a number for each of your fingers (or you can draw the numbers on). From left to right, start with the number 1 for the little finger of your left hand, 2 for your left ring finger, and so on. Be sure to include your thumbs in the count. You will end with the number 10 on the little finger of your right hand.

The Routine

1. Now you can multiply nine times any number from 1 to 10. For example, to multiply 9 × 2 bend the number 2 finger (the ring finger of your left hand). Count how many fingers are on each side of it. One is on the left side, and eight on the right. 1 next to 8 makes the number 18. There's your answer.

2. Let's try another. To multiply 9 × 7 bend the number 7 finger (the first finger of your right hand). Count the fingers on either side of it: 6 on the left, and 3 on the right. The answer is 63.

The Secret

Bend in whichever number-finger that you are multiplying nine by, then count how many fingers are on either side of it. Those are the numbers exactly as they would appear on a calculator!

HANDHELD COMPUTER

THANKS, BORIS... I CAN ALWAYS COUNT ON YOU!

This is a very old Russian method of multiplying numbers from 6 to 10. It's fast and easy to learn, and works by breaking the multiplication down into small parts (of easier multiplication and addition).

☞ Materials

Pen (optional)

☞ Preparation

Follow this numbering plan for each hand:

Thumb = 10
Index finger = 9
Middle finger = 8
Ring finger = 7
Little finger = 6

The Routine

1. Suppose you want to multiply 7 by 8. Touch the tip of the 7-finger (on either hand) against the tip of the 8-finger of the other hand. The touching fingers, together with all the fingers below them on both hands, represent tens. In this case, there are 5 fingers. Five tens are 50.

2. The next step is to multiply the number of remaining fingers on the left hand by the number of remaining fingers on the right. In this case, 3 times 2 equals 6.

3. Now, add 6 to 50 to obtain the final answer: 56. It works every time!

SPEEDY ARITHMETIC

This trick will turn you into a lightning-fast adding machine.

⚡ The Effect

You and a volunteer take turns writing down five-digit numbers, one beneath the other. After writing down the fifth five-digit number, you draw a line under it and instantly add them all up correctly. More startling, you write the total from left to right!

☜ Materials

Paper
Pens

The Secret

Your volunteer writes down the first five-digit number. When you write down the next number, make sure that each digit in your number, when added to the one above it, will total nine.

For example:

Volunteer's number: 37854
Your number: 62145

Ask your volunteer to write down another five-digit number below these two. You write the next five-digit number, following the same nine-principle. After your volunteer writes down the fifth five-digit number, draw a line under it. Here's how to find the total:

Subtract 2 from the fifth digit of the number your volunteer just wrote, and put 2 in front of what's left.

For example:

Volunteer's number: 37854
Your number: 62145
Volunteer's number: 42896
Your number: 57103
Volunteer's number: 23789

Subtracting 2 from the fifth digit of the last number leaves 23787. Placing a 2 in front of that gives us the final answer: 223787.

ARITH-MAGIC

This is a very simple trick where you can reveal a number that someone is merely thinking about. You can use the idea behind it for many similar tricks.

🎩 The Effect

Your spectator thinks of a low number and does some arithmetic on it. You will always know the final number your spectator has in mind.

To prove that the answer doesn't always turn out the same, you repeat the trick twice! The third time, your spectator will be sure that you're stumped because they'll be thinking of a fraction. As always, you know the answer.

The Routine and Patter

1. Ask your spectator to think of any number. Since this will involve some mental arithmetic, tell your spectator to pick a number less than 10.

2. Ask you spectator to double the number, and then add 8.

3. Now divide the new number by 2.

4. Finally, subtract the original number (the first one your spectator thought up).

5. At this point, it's a good idea to recap everything that just happened. Say, "You thought of any number, then mixed it up by doubling it and doing some adding and subtracting and dividing. I think I'm getting an image of your number: The answer is 4!"

The Secret

The final answer to this trick will always be half of whatever number you ask them to add to their original number. In the description above, we used the number 8, so the final answer will be 4. If we had used the number 10, the final answer would have been 5.

Your spectator can think up any number at all. It doesn't matter what number they choose because at the end of the trick you have them subtract that number at the end. You don't need to know what that number is because it comes and goes without changing the other bit of math that happens in between.

You can also use this idea for any trick where you need the spectator to arrive at a particular number. You "insert" this little routine into another trick very easily.

Let's try an example:

Let's say your spectator chooses the number 7.

First they double it: $7 \times 2 = 14$.

Then let's say you have them add 4 to it: $14 + 4 = 18$.

Then they divide this number by two: $18 \div 2 = 9$.

Finally, they subtract their original number: $9 - 7 = 2$.

Two is half of the number you asked them to add at the beginning!

It's always good to do some kind of patter at the end before revealing the final number. It will distract your spectator from thinking too closely about the addition, subtraction, multiplication, and division they just did.

This is one of the few tricks that you can (and really should) repeat. The answer only depends on the number that you ask them to add in at the beginning. It can be different each time.

A good kicker (a finishing version, for the final time you do this for someone) is to have them add in an odd number at the beginning. That way, the final answer will always be a fraction.

For example:

Let's say they think up the number 4.

First they double it: $4 \times 2 = 8$.

Then let's say you have them add 3 (remember half of 3 is 1½):

$8 + 3 = 11$.

Then they divide this by 2: $11 \div 2 = 5½$.

And finally, they subtract their original number: $5½ - 4 = 1½$.

I'VE GOT HALF A MIND TO DO THESE TRICKS!

I GET YOUR POINT !!

Your spectator will be sure that they've "got" you because the final answer is a fraction. As with most magic tricks, here's where your acting skills come into play. You can play with their misconceptions for a while before finally revealing the final answer.

STRANGE MULTIPLICATION

There are many ways to multiply numbers that have more than one digit. Here's one of the weirdest.

☞ Materials

Paper
Pen
A calculator

The Routine

1. Let's say you want to multiply 23 by 17. On a piece of paper, write 23, and then write 17 next to it. Leave some space between them because you'll be writing down a column of numbers underneath each one. We'll call the 23 the left-side column, and the 17 the right-side column.

2. Under the 23: Half of 23 is 11½. Ignore the fraction and write 11 under 23. Half of 11 is 5½. Again ignore the fraction, and write 5 under the 11. Create a column of numbers underneath the 23 that are made up by dividing each successive number by 2 and omitting any remainders. Continue until you reach the number 1.

3. Under the 17: Double each number to obtain the one below. Continue until you have a matching number for each one in the left-side column.

4. Here comes the weird part. Cross out any row that has an even number in the left-side column. In this example, there is only one. Now add up all the numbers remaining in the right-side column. Believe it or not, the final answer will be the product of 23 and 17!

23	17	
11	34	
5	68	
2	136	(Cross this one out because it has an even
1	272	number in the left side column)

Add up the remaining numbers in the right-side column:

$$
\begin{array}{r}
17 \\
34 \\
68 \\
\underline{272} \\
391
\end{array}
$$

MULTIPLICATION MAGIC

Here's another fun way to reveal a number that your spectator thinks up. It may help to have a calculator handy for this one, but if your spectator is good at multiplication, it might be more interesting to have them work it out on paper.

🎩 The Effect

You show your spectator a huge "magic" number. Your spectator thinks up any single-digit number and tells it to you. You have them multiply the magic number by another different number, and the final answer is a row of digits identical to the one they thought of at the beginning.

👈 Materials
Paper
Pen
A calculator

The Routine

1. Write down the "magic" number 12345679. It's easy to remember because it consists of all the digits from one to nine, in order, with the number eight left out.

2. Now ask your spectator to tell you any single-digit number (any number from 1 to 9). To yourself, multiply this number by 9 and write the answer down under the "magic" number.

3. Have your spectator multiply the magic number by the one you just wrote down.

Here's an example:

Let's say your spectator chooses the number 7. As quickly as you can, multiply 7×9 and write down the answer underneath the "magic" number. In this case the answer is 63.

$12345679 \times 63 = 777777777$

This trick works best when it's done quickly. The effect is quite startling, and works for any single-digit number.

DIABOLICAL DICE (PART I)

After seeing this trick, your friends will believe that you have X-ray vision!

🎩 The Effect

Your spectator rolls a pair of dice, stacks them, and adds up the three sides that aren't showing (the bottom side of the top die, the top and bottom sides of the bottom die). Without looking, you can tell them the total.

☞ Materials

Paper
Pen
A pair of dice

The Routine

1. Have your spectator roll the dice several times to make sure that they aren't "loaded" (that they don't roll the same numbers all the time).

2. Turn away from the audience. Ask your spectator to roll the dice one more time, then set one die on top of the other. Turn around briefly to make sure the dice are squared up and stacked properly, then turn away again.

3. What you're really doing when you turn around is taking a quick peek at the number showing on the top die. Subtract this number from 14, and write it on the piece of paper. Fold the paper and place it on the table.

4. Tell the audience that there are three sides to the dice that no one can see right now: one is against the tabletop, and two are touching each other. Ask the spectator to carefully lift the dice and add those three hidden sides.

5. Now you can take all the time you want to play up the drama before revealing the number you wrote down.

The Secret

Most people don't know that the two opposing sides of a die always add up to seven. So, if you add up the opposing sides of two dice, the answer is 14. When you turned around to make sure the dice were stacked correctly, you peeked at the top number. Subtracting that from 14 gives you the total of the three hidden sides.

A good "kicker' is to introduce one more die at the end of the trick. Tell the audience it's hard enough to predict the roll of the dice when there are two, but imagine how hard it is with three.

Perform the trick as before. This time, subtract the top number from 21 (7 × 3). With three stacked dice, there are five sides hidden from view. Have the spectator add those up, and they will match your prediction.

Of course, you can use any number of dice for this trick. Multiply the number of dice by 7 for the number you need to keep in mind. With three dice, subtract the top number of the stacked dice from 21. With four dice, subtract the number from 28. With five dice, subtract it from 35, and so on. With more dice, you'll have a better excuse for turning around to "check that the dice are stacked correctly."

DIABOLICAL DICE (PART II)

This trick is a great follow-up to the previous one. It works with two dice, but it's more effective with three.

🎩 The Effect
Your spectator rolls three dice, some of them more than once, and adds up several of the sides. Without looking at the dice, you know the total.

CAREFUL...THIS TRICK CAN BE DICEY!

🖙 Materials
Three dice

The Routine and Patter

1. While you're turned away from the audience, have your spectator roll the three dice. Have them add up the three numbers that they've rolled (they shouldn't say this number out loud).

2. Ask you spectator to carefully pick up any one of the three dice and add the number on the bottom of it to the total.

3. Finally, have your spectator roll that same die, and add the number they rolled to the total.

4. Face the audience. Pick up all three dice and put them away, or to one side.

5. As you pick them up, nonchalantly (and secretly) look at the three numbers showing, add them up, and add another 7 to the total. This is the number that your spectator has in mind.

6. It's a good idea to recap what your spectator did. The patter (and removing the dice) will help to hide what you are actually doing.

You can say, "You are now thinking of a number that you came up with by adding several numbers from several completely random throws of three dice. Concentrate on your number."

And then you reveal it!

The Secret

As with the previous trick, this one works because the top and bottom of any die add up to 7. Also as before, you can use as many dice as you like. Three is probably the best: it seems more "random" than two dice, and the math is easier to handle than with four or more dice.

PAPER CALCULATOR

This is an easy and fun bit of mental magic that also involves some cool props.

YOU'RE SUCH A CARD!

THANKS!

The Effect

Your spectator thinks of any number from 1 to 63. You show seven cards with various numbers written on them. Your volunteer hands you the cards with their chosen number on it. Instantly, you reveal their number.

Materials

Six index or business cards
Pen

Preparation

On six index cards, write down the numbers on pages 36–37. If you want to carry these around in you wallet, you can also write these numbers on the back of six business cards. This might take a few tries to get them spaced correctly. Make sure you write neatly and leave enough space between the numbers so you can read them.

Card 1:

1	3	5	7	9	11	13
15	17	19	21	23	25	27
29	31	33	35	37	39	41
43	45	47	49	51	53	55
57	59	61	63			

Card 2:

2	3	6	7	10	11	14
15	18	19	22	23	26	27
30	31	34	35	38	39	42
43	46	47	50	51	54	55
58	59	62	63			

Card 3:

4	5	6	7	12	13	14
15	20	21	22	23	28	29
30	31	36	37	38	39	44
45	46	47	52	53	54	55
60	61	62	63			

Card 4:

8	9	10	11	12	13	14
15	24	25	26	27	28	29
30	31	40	41	42	43	44
45	46	47	56	57	58	59
60	61	62	63			

Card 5:

16	17	18	19	20	21	22
23	24	25	26	27	28	29
30	31	48	49	50	51	52
53	54	55	56	57	58	59
60	61	62	63			

Card 6:

32	33	34	35	36	37	38
39	40	41	42	43	44	45
46	47	48	49	50	51	52
53	54	55	56	57	58	59
60	61	62	63			

The Routine and Patter

1. Ask your spectator to think of a number between 1 and 63. Give them the six cards and ask them to hand you every card that has their number on it.

2. As they hand you the cards, secretly add up each number that's in the top left corner. The total will always equal the number they thought up. This is the fast way to do this trick.

3. You can also make up a story about the cards to make it more interesting. For example, you can say, "Before there were the kind of computers we have now, people used punch cards. These were little manila cards with holes punched in them to transmit information. These six cards are versions of the old punch cards and I know how to read them like the old computers did." Then you tell them the answer.

MAGIC²

Magic squares are old mathematical puzzles that you can use to create this magic trick. In a magic square, the numbers in any row (across, vertically, or diagonally) always add up to the same number. Magic squares always use a sequence of numbers, which means a group of numbers that follow some kind of regular order.

🎩 The Effect

You draw two tic-tac-toe boxes and give one to someone in the audience. You can also do this on a blackboard. You explain what a magic square is and that this will be a race between you and the other person to create one. You ask the audience to call out the numbers 1 to 9 in any order. As each number is called out, you and the person write the number in one of your boxes. When the last number is called out, you're the first to create a perfect magic square!

☞ Materials

Paper
Pens
Blackboard and chalk (optional)

☞ Preparation

All you'll need for this trick is to study the magic square provided on the next page, or come up with your own from the instructions on pages 41–42.

The Secret

There are a two ways to do this trick. The easiest is to memorize this magic square:

4	9	2
3	5	7
8	1	6

In this magic square, the numbers in any row add up to 15.

The harder way to do the trick is to make up your own magic square. You can repeat this trick with a different-looking square each time. The secret is that you can rotate the square and the numbers will still add up to 15.

Here's one rotation (clockwise):

8	3	4
1	5	9
6	7	2

Here's one more rotation:

6	1	8
7	5	3
2	9	4

Finally, here's one last rotation:

2	7	6
9	5	1
4	3	8

If you rotated this square once more, you would have the same square that we had at the beginning of this trick.

Another Square

This square uses all the numbers from 4 to 12 so that the rows, columns, and diagonal lines add up to 24:

11	4	9
6	8	10
7	12	5

If you can also remember this square, then you can extend this trick even further. Draw up another empty magic square and this time ask the audience to call out numbers in any order from 4 to 12. As soon as the last number is called out, you've completed the magic square.

Super Square

If the previous squares didn't amaze your math teacher, this one definitely will. It's a five-by-five magic square that uses every number from 1 to 25. Every row, column, and diagonal line adds up to 65:

1	24	17	15	8
14	7	5	23	16
22	20	13	6	4
10	3	21	19	12
18	11	9	2	25

This super square is pretty hard to memorize, so it might be easier to write this down and keep it hidden in your hand for the trick. If you hold a handful of papers in one hand, you can hide this on the top or bottom of the paper and sneak peeks at it during the trick.

To make your own three-by-three magic square, come up with a sequence of nine numbers. The numbers have to be in some kind of regular order. For example, the trick described on pages 38–39 uses the numbers in order from 1 to 9. You could also choose a sequence that goes by twos (2, 4, 6, 8, 10, 12, 14, 16, 18) or by fives (5, 10, 15, 20, 25, 30, 35, 40, 45).

Find the number that falls in the exact middle of your sequence of numbers. In the sequence from 1 to 9, that middle number is 5. In the sequence from 2 to 18 (going by twos), the middle number is 10. In the sequence from 5 to 45 (going by fives), the middle number is 25.

1, 2, 3, 4, 5, 6, 7, 8, 9	—Middle number is 5
2, 4, 6, 8, 10, 12, 14, 16, 18	—Middle number is 10
5, 10, 15, 20, 25, 30, 35, 40, 45	—Middle number is 25

Take this middle number and write it in the center square.

Take the very first number in your sequence and write it somewhere else in the square.

Take the very last number in your sequence and write it in the square directly opposite from where you wrote the very first number in your sequence. For example, if you put the first number in the top left square, the last number would go in the bottom right square.

You should now have one complete row. Add up the numbers in the row and remember the result. This number is the key to completing the magic square.

Fill in the other spaces with the remaining numbers, making sure that every row, column, and diagonal sequence adds up to the same result.

MAGIC BY THE MONTH

This trick utilizes two little-known mathematical facts about calendars. Once you've learned them, you'll be able to perform this trick with any monthly calendar.

🎩 The Effect

Have your audience choose dates at random from a calendar page. When they add up these numbers, the result matches a prediction you made before the trick even started!

☞Materials

A page from a monthly calendar (the entire month must be on one page)
A magic marker

The Routine

1. Hand the calendar page and marker to someone in your audience. Ask them to mark off a four-by-four square of dates anywhere on the calendar.

2. As soon as they do this, secretly make note of the numbers in two opposite corners of the square. For example, the numbers in the upper left and lower right corners, or the numbers in the upper right and lower left corners. Add these two numbers together and multiply the result by 2. Remember this number.

3. Tell your audience you're going to make a prediction. Write the number you came up with on a slip of paper, fold it up several times, and give it to someone in the audience to hold on to until the end of the trick.

4. Turn away from the audience. Ask your volunteer to circle any date in the square. Then have them cross out every other date in the same row, horizontally and vertically.

5. Ask them to keep doing this until every date in the square is either circled or crossed out.

6. Ask someone else to add up all the circled numbers. Turn around and have your prediction read out loud. The numbers will match!

The Secret

This trick works automatically. There are two mathematical secrets behind it:

1. On a monthly calendar page, if you mark off a four-by-four square of dates, the sum of the numbers in the upper left and lower right corners will always equal the sum of the numbers in the other two corners.

2. If you circle and cross off dates as described above, the circled numbers will always equal the sum of the numbers in each corner.

THE ADDING GRID

This trick combines some of the principles used in Magic² and Magic by the Month.

🎩 The Effect

You show your audience a five-by-five grid. Each square in the grid has a number in it. You also have a handful of coins for the audience to use.

While you're turned away, you ask them to cover a number with a coin and then cross out all the numbers in the same row with it, across and down.

When all the numbers are either covered with coins or crossed out, you can tell the audience the sum of all the covered numbers. (Based on the example on the next page, the answer is 94.)

☞ Materials

A grid of numbers (see next page)
Coins that are large enough to cover one of the boxes in the grid
A magic marker

The Secret

To describe this trick, we can use this grid as an example. The grid does not include the numbers in parentheses, but they are very important.

	(3)	(13)	(11)	(14)	(6)
(1)	4	14	12	15	7
(30)	33	43	41	44	36
(8)	11	21	19	22	14
(7)	10	20	18	21	13
(1)	4	14	12	15	7

In this grid, each number is the sum of the numbers in parentheses that line up with it. For example, if you line up the numbers in parentheses (13) and (8), you'll find the number 21 in the grid. If you line up the numbers (14) and (8), you'll find the number 22.

☞Preparation

It's very easy to make one of these grids yourself. For this trick, it's useful to make several grids. That way, you can show them all at the beginning of the trick and your audience can choose one, making the numbers seem to be even more "random."

The Routine

1. First, pick a "key" number. This will end up as half of the sum of all the covered numbers in the trick. Any two-digit number will work perfectly. In the example grid, the key number is 47, and the answer will be 94.

2. To remember the number, write the first digit of the key number in the upper left corner of the grid. Write the second digit in the lower right corner.

3. Outside of the square (represented here in parentheses), write two numbers that will add up to each of those digits. In the example, you can see (3) and (1) line up for the 4, and (6) and (1) line up for the 7.

4. Write any numbers along the rest of the line outside of the square. You can use any numbers as long as they will all add up to your key number.

5. In the example, across the top the bracketed numbers add up this way: 3 + 13 + 11 + 14 + 6 = 47. They also add up down the side: 1 + 30 + 8 + 7 + 1 = 47.

6. Now you can fill in the grid by adding up the numbers outside of the square.

7. If you create several of these grids, you can always remember the key number by looking at the digits in the upper left and lower right corners.

If you perform the routine as described, the results will always work!

WEIRD NUMBER∫

This trick is actually made up of four different, weird facts about numbers. Once you've performed it, your friends will be convinced that you're an expert with numbers.

🎩 The Effect

Tell your audience about several strange numbers. Ask them to add and multiply the numbers in different ways in order to create four weird effects.

☞ Materials

Pencils
Paper
A calculator

The Routine

Weird Effect #1:

1. Give out the pencils and paper, and ask your audience to add, then multiply these pairs of numbers: 9 and

9, 24 and 3, 47 and 2, 497 and 2. Ask them to examine their answers and see if there are any strange relationships happening.

9 + 9 = 18	9 × 9 = 81
24 + 3 = 27	24 × 3 = 72
47 + 2 = 49	47 × 2 = 94
497 + 2 = 499	497 × 2 = 944

The answers in the addition side are the exact reverse of the answers in the multiplication side!

Weird Effect #2:

1. Tell your audience that a very weird number is 37. Ask them to multiply it by 1, by 2, by 3, all the way up to 9, and write down each of the answers.

2. Have them multiply each answer by 3. This strange sequence will appear:

111, 222, 333, 444, 555, 666, 777, 888, 999.

Weird Effect #3:

1. Another weird number is 12345679 (notice that the 8 isn't there). Ask your audience to multiply this number by every number from 1 to 9, and to write down each of the answers.

2. Have them multiply each of the answers by 9, and they'll find this weird group of numbers:

111111111, 222222222, 333333333,
444444444, 555555555, 666666666,
777777777, 888888888, 999999999.

Weird Effect #4:

1. This time the weird number is 142857. Ask part of your audience to multiply this number by 2, 3, 4, 5, and

6, and to write down the answers. Ask the other part of your audience to multiply it by 7, 14, and 21.

2. When everyone's ready, ask the first group to add up all the digits in each of their answers. They'll find that the digits in each number will add up to 27.

3. Ask the second group to do the same. They'll find that the digits in each of their answers will add up to 54, which is what you get when you multiply 27 times 2!

4. Tell your audience that this magic number (142857) has two other weird properties.

5. Ask them to look at the first digits in all of the answers that they came up with by multiplying the magic number by 2, 3, 4, 5, and 6. The first digit gets bigger with each answer, and they are all contained in the original weird number itself.

The weirdest thing about this number is that the first group of answers contains the same digits in the same order of the original number. It is as if the original weird number is on a loop and is rotating along one digit further each time.

$142857 \times 2 = 285714$ $2 + 8 + 5 + 7 + 1 + 4 = 27$
$142857 \times 3 = 428571$ $4 + 2 + 8 + 5 + 7 + 1 = 27$
$142857 \times 4 = 571428$ $5 + 7 + 1 + 4 + 2 + 8 = 27$
$142857 \times 5 = 714285$ $7 + 1 + 4 + 2 + 8 + 5 = 27$
$142857 \times 6 = 857142$ $8 + 5 + 7 + 1 + 4 + 2 = 27$

$142857 \times 7 = 999999$ $9 + 9 + 9 + 9 + 9 + 9 = 54$
                                   (which $= 27 \times 2$)
$142857 \times 14 = 1999998$ $1 + 9 + 9 + 9 + 9 + 9 + 8 = 54$
$142857 \times 21 = 2999997$ $2 + 9 + 9 + 9 + 9 + 9 + 7 = 54$

2.
MAGIC WITH CARDS

THE 21 CARDS

SORRY KID!...
YOU GOTTA BE
21 TO PLAY
THIS GAME!

21 CARDS

This is one of the world's most famous card tricks. One of the reasons for its popularity is that the spectator only has to think of a card, rather than picking it from the deck. It originated in the 18th century, and over the years, several different versions have appeared. Some versions use as few as nine cards, others as many as twenty-seven. This is the basic method.

🎩 The Effect

Put a group of cards on the table and then ask a friend to think of one of them. You gather the cards and deal them twice. Then you identify the chosen card.

☞ Materials

Twenty-one playing cards

☜ Preparation

None! One of the strengths of this trick is that it works all by itself.

The Routine and Patter

1. Deal three cards faceup onto the table. Place them an inch apart in a single row.

2. Deal another row faceup on top of the first row, but place them about halfway down on the first row of cards. Deal five more rows the same way.

3. You should end up with three columns of cards. Each column should have seven cards (twenty-one cards in all). We'll call the left-hand column A, the middle column B, and the right-hand column C.

4. Say: "Think of one of the cards you see on the table. Don't touch it or tell me which one. Just think of it. Let me know when you have one."

I COULD USE A 7 UP!

5. Square up all the cards in column A into a faceup pile. Do the same for column B, then column C.

6. Say, "Don't tell me which card you thought of. I just need to know which pile it's in."

7. Pick up that pile and drop it faceup on top of one of the other piles. Pick up the remaining pile and drop it on top of the stack. The chosen pile of cards should now be sandwiched between the other two.

8. Pick up the entire stack of twenty-one cards and turn it facedown.

9. Repeat steps 1 through 3: dealing out the cards, asking the spectator which pile their card is in and sandwiching that pile between the other two.

10. Finally, repeat steps 1 and 2. Now, when your spectator tells you which column the card is in, you'll know their chosen card right away. It's always the fourth card down in the column. You can find their card just by mentally counting down to it.

11. At this point in the trick, there are a lot of ways to reveal the card. The least dramatic way would be to point to their card on the table. Here's the most famous method:

After your spectator tells you which pile their card is in, repeat step 3: sandwiching that pile between the other two. Now the chosen card is eleven cards down from the top. Give the stack of twenty-one cards to the spectator.

Say, "We need a magic spell to make this trick work. Can you spell out the words 'Magic Spell,' and deal out one card facedown for each letter?"

After they do this, have the spectator turn over the next card (the eleventh). Ta-daa! It's their card!

THAT'S AMAZING!

You can use any ten- or eleven-letter word to discover their card, such as "Abracadabra" (eleven letters), or "Hocus-pocus" (ten letters). A very powerful method would be to use the spectator's own name, if their name has ten or eleven letters in it.

ODDS AND EVENS

This trick involves "stacking the deck," which means to prearrange the cards secretly before you perform.

🎩 The Effect

You cut the deck into two piles. While your back is turned, a card is chosen from each pile and replaced in the opposite pile. Then the spectator shuffles each pile. You are able to find their cards immediately.

A NINE OF HEARTS?!.. HOW ODD!

👈 Materials

A deck of playing cards

☞Preparation

Divide the deck of cards into a pile of even-numbered cards and a pile of odd-numbered cards. The Ace counts as 1, the Jack is 11, the Queen is 12, and the King is 13. The beauty of this "stack" is that on first glance, the cards don't look prearranged at all.

The Routine

1. Square up the cards and hold the two sections together as if you are going to deal them out. Secretly keep your little finger in the gap between the two sections. Casually pretend to cut the deck by just lifting off the top half (above your little finger). Place the two piles on the table and you're ready to begin.

This trick is most effective when you have two spectators helping you, but you can also have one person choose two cards. With two spectators, hand them each one pile of cards and ask them to shuffle each pile.

2. Turn around and ask your spectator to choose a card from their pile (you can call it a mini-deck). Ask them to remember their card and place it into the other person's mini-deck.

3. Have them shuffle their cards. Then place one mini-deck on top of the other and square them all up.

4. Turn around to face the audience and recap what just happened: you cut the deck in half and two cards were chosen—one from each half. The deck has been shuffled and all of this took place while you weren't even looking.

5. While you're giving your recap, pick up the deck and look through the cards. You will find one odd-numbered card in the half full of even-numbered cards and one even-numbered card in the half full of odd-numbered ones.

6. The best way to reveal this is to take out each card and place them facedown on the table. Have your spectators tell you the cards they chose. Turn them over at the same time and accept your well-deserved applause.

FROM ONE END TO ANOTHER

Here's a trick that uses a "stack" of cards for a very unique effect. You can also repeat this one several times.

♟ The Effect
You deal out a row of cards. While your back is turned, a spectator moves a number of cards from one end of the row to another. You turn around and magically figure out how many cards were moved.

☞Materials
A deck of playing cards

☞Preparation
Take out the Joker and ten cards in order from Ace through 10. The suits don't matter. Deal them out face-down and in order from left to right: Joker, Ace, 2, 3, 4, 5, 6, 7, 8, 9, 10.

The Routine

1. Ask your spectator to move any number of cards one at a time *from one end of the row to the other*. Demonstrate by moving a few from the right-hand side to the left. It is very important that you remember how many you moved.

2. Turn around and ask your spectator to move some cards just as you demonstrated. They should move them

from the same side as you did. They can move any number, from one to ten cards.

3. Turn around and face the audience. Perform some hocus-pocus, such as waving your hands over the cards.

4. Remember how many cards you moved earlier. Count that number over from the right-hand side of the row. Lift up that card, glance at it, and replace it. The number on that card is the number of cards that your spectator moved. Lift up a few other cards as if you're in deep concentration, or as if you're unsure of what you're doing. Then reveal the number.

5. You can gather up the cards, put them in order again, and repeat the trick, if you like. Make sure to move a few cards yourself at the beginning, as a demonstration.

CALCULATOR CARDS

This is a card trick that doesn't even need a deck of cards!

... I PLAN EVERY MOVE!...

...HE'S SO CALCULATING!

The Effect

Your spectator thinks of a card and performs a few calculations. You are immediately able to reveal the chosen card.

Materials

Paper
Pen
A deck of playing cards
A calculator

☞ Preparation

On a piece of paper, write down the following chart:

Ace = 1	Clubs = 1
Jack = 11	Diamonds = 2
Queen = 12	Hearts = 3
King = 13	Spades = 4

The Routine

1. Ask your spectator to think of a card and write it down.

2. Give your spectator the calculator and tell them to enter the card's number.

3. Add the number that is one more than their number.

4. Multiply the result by 5.

5. Add the value of the suit to that number.

6. Add 637 to the result. Ask your spectator to give you the calculator with the final result showing.

7. To find their card, simply subtract 642. The first number (or two numbers, if it's three digits long) equals the number value of their card. The last number is the suit value.

HOW'D YOU GET TO BE SUCH A BIG NUMBER?

...I EIGHT TOO MUCH

INCOMPLETE PREDICTION

This trick seems to go wrong until you produce the surprise ending.

OKAY... DON'T TELL ME!
YOU'VE GOT DIAMONDS
IN YOUR SUIT ?!...

WOW!

🎩 The Effect

You write down a prediction of what card your spectator will choose. Your spectator chooses a number at random and counts down that many cards in the deck. At first, your prediction doesn't match. Then you make a few "adjustments" to your prediction and the name of the card appears.

☞ Materials

A deck of playing cards
Paper
Pen
A calculator

☞ Preparation

Make sure the ten of hearts is the eighteenth card down from the top of the deck.

The Routine

1. On a piece of paper write "The name of the card is." Fold the paper and tell your audience that this is your prediction. Leave this paper in plain view for the whole trick.

2. Ask your spectator to think of a three-digit number. The first digit should be larger than the last digit. Have the spectator (or another person) enter that number into the calculator.

3. Ask your spectator to reverse the three digits and subtract that number from the first one. (This is why the first digit had to be larger than the last one.)

4. Ask the spectator to add up the digits in the answer and to count down that number of cards in the deck. Have them remove the eighteenth card and show it to everyone, then have them open your prediction and read it out loud.

5. Tell your audience that you were in such a hurry you forgot to complete your prediction. Take the paper and pen and cross out the following letters:

- The H in THE
- The AME in NAME
- The T in the second THE
- The C and D in CARD
- Change the I in IS to a T by drawing a line across the top of it.

The remaining letters spell "Ten of Hearts."

The Secret

The answer to the arithmetic you asked your spectator to do will always equal 18.

For example, say your spectator chose the number 942.

942 − 249 = 693

6 + 9 + 3 = 18

You know the answer will always equal 18, so you place your predicted card at that position in the deck.

This trick works with part of the principle used in the first trick, "One Thousand Eighty-Nine" (see page 9). You can use this principle for many other tricks. Try to invent your own routine based on it.

STACKING THE DECK

This trick uses arithmetic and some sneaky planning on your part to get the spectator to unwittingly stack the deck for you.

The Effect

You write down a prediction of what card will be chosen. Your spectator picks four cards at random, performs some arithmetic based on these, and ends up picking a card that matches your prediction.

Materials

A deck of playing cards
Paper
Pen

The Routine

1. Ask your spectator to shuffle the cards and hand them to you. As you square them up, take a look at the bottom card and remember it. The easiest way to do this without making it obvious is to have them hand it to you faceup, or look through the deck to remove the Jokers.

2. Write the name of this card on a piece of paper and fold it up so your spectator can't see it. Say that this is your prediction and leave it in view for the whole trick.

3. Deal twelve cards facedown in a row. Ask your spectator to choose any four of them. Turn those faceup and gather the remaining eight cards. These go on the bottom of the deck.

4. Give the deck to your spectator and ask them to deal cards facedown beneath each of the four cards they chose. They should start with the number on a faceup card and deal out however many cards it takes to reach the number 10.

For example if the faceup card is a 6, the spectator should deal out four cards in a column beneath it. Face cards are already worth 10, and Aces equal 1.

5. Ask your spectator to gather up all the facedown cards and put them on the bottom of the deck.

6. Ask your spectator to add up the number value of the four faceup cards. Deal down that number from the top of the deck. The card at that position will match your prediction.

The Presentation

It will seem mighty suspicious to your spectator to have all these cards dealt and then gathered up again for no apparent reason. Make up a story to go with this routine.

For example, you can talk about a magic game of solitaire, which involves dealing cards out in the manner described above. Once the cards are all dealt out, ask your spectator to gather them into piles, then stack one pile on top of another. You can even ask the spectator to stack the piles in a particular order, say, least number of cards to most. Finally place the deck on top of them and continue with the trick.

3.
MAGIC WITH COINS

THE SHEEP AND THE WOLVES

This is an old coin routine that is fast, simple, and surprising. It works because people lose track of the number of coins on the table and in your hands.

🎩 The Effect

You're telling a story about wolves trying to steal sheep (represented by some coins). The coins appear to be divided equally between the wolves, but at the end of the trick all of the sheep coins are in one hand and the wolf coins are in the other.

PICK A COIN!.. DON'T BE SHEEPISH!

THIS COULD BE BAAADD!!

☞ Materials

Seven coins of the same value

The Routine and Patter

1. Lay the seven coins in a row on a table. Pick up one coin in each hand and show them on your open palms. Say, "There once were these two wolves."

2. Show the coin in your left hand and say, "This is Fred." Show the coin in your right hand and say, "This is Ned." (Of course, you can come up with your own names, or even invent your own story for this routine.) "They were hiding behind some trees one day when they saw five sheep in a field. Fred said to Ned, 'Let's go steal those sheep.'"

3. Close your hands into fists, hiding the "wolves" from view. Pick up one of the sheep coins with your left hand. Then pick up one with your right. Quickly, pick up the coins back and forth between your hands until you have them all.

4. Keep your hands closed so the audience can't see how many you're really holding in each hand. You should have more in your left hand than in your right. Continue your story by saying, "Fred said to Ned, 'Did you hear something? I think that sheepdog is coming back. Let's put these back and wait until he's gone.'"

5. Without opening your fists, slide one coin out of your right hand and put it on the table. Do the same with one from your left hand. Keep going back and forth until there are five coins on the table.

6. Keep both hands closed as if you're still holding coins in both of them. Your right hand should be empty. Say, "They waited a while but never saw a sheep dog."

7. Shake your right hand and say, "Ned said, 'Fred.'" Shake your left fist. "'You dummy. There never was a sheepdog. Let's steal those sheep and get back home right away.'"

8. Starting with your left hand, quickly pick up the coins from the table, going back and forth until you have them all. Your right hand should have two coins and your left hand should have five. Finish your story by saying, "They picked up the sheep and ran back home. But there was a problem. The sheepdog really was there, and he followed them home. As Fred and Ned set the sheep down to open their front door, the sheepdog picked the sheep up and whisked them back to the field."

9. Open your right hand to show the two coins. The audience will believe these are the "wolves."

10. Open your left hand to show the five "sheep."

COIN ROWS

Here's a fun trick you can do with all of those extra coins you find in your pockets.

🎩 The Effect

While your back is turned, your spectator lays out some coins on the table and then removes some of them. You are able to figure out exactly how many are left behind.

☞ Materials

Twenty to thirty coins of the same value

The Routine

1. While your back is turned, ask your spectator to choose an odd number of coins from the pile and lay them out in two rows. The top row should have one more coin than the bottom row.

2. Ask your spectator to call out a number that is greater than zero, but less than the number of coins in the top row. (Remember this number. It's very important.) Ask your spectator to remove that number of coins from the top row.

3. Have your spectator silently count the number of coins left in the top row and then remove that number of coins from the bottom row.

4. Ask your spectator to remove the remaining coins in the top row and to concentrate on the number of coins left on the table.

5. Recap to your audience what has happened: an unknown number of coins was chosen and then several of them were taken away. Immediately, you can announce how many coins are left.

The Secret

When your spectator tells you the first number of coins removed from the top row, simply subtract one from it. That will always equal the number of coins left over at the end.

DOES THIS TRICK ALWAYS WORK?

COUNT ON IT!

A FISTFUL OF COINS

Here's a useful fact about numbers with more than one digit: if you add up all the digits of a number and subtract the total from the original number, the answer will always be a multiple of nine. This amazing mind-reading trick is based on that fact.

🎩 The Effect

While your back is turned, your spectator removes various numbers of coins from the table, puts some away, and keeps some in their fist. You turn around and instantly tell them how many coins are in their hand.

👉 Materials

Twenty coins

The Routine

1. Put all the coins on the table and then turn away. Ask your spectator to follow these instructions:

   a. Take any number of coins, from one to ten, and put them away.

   b. Count the remaining coins on the table. Add the two digits together and remove the number of coins that correspond to that number. For example, if there are sixteen coins left on the table, then 1 + 6 = 7; so your spectator should take away seven coins. Put these seven coins away.

   c. Pick up any number of the remaining coins and hold them in a fist.

2. When you turn around, you will know how many they are holding.

The Secret

Step b will always leave nine coins.

When you turn around, count the coins left on the table and subtract that number from nine. The result will equal the number of coins the spectator is holding. It works every time!

THE STICKY COIN

This quick trick makes use of inertia. That's what you call it when objects at rest resist being made to move.

🎩 The Effect
You place a large coin on an index card and balance it on the end of your finger. With a fast flick, the card is gone, but the coin appears to have stuck to your finger.

☞ Materials
An index card (or playing card)
A coin (the larger the better)

The Routine
1. Place the coin on the card and then place them both on the end of your index finger with your hand held palm-up.

2. With your other hand, flick the edge of the card nearest to you. You'll have to practice this a bit to find the best position for your hands and the right amount of force. The card should fly away, leaving the coin balanced on the end of your finger.

The Secret
The trick depends on the inertia of the coin. By flicking at the card, you're putting it into motion very quickly. The coin is heavier and has more inertia, so it resists being set in motion.

4.
MAGIC WITH
SHAPES

MÖBIUS STRIPS

Magicians sometimes call this trick the Afghan Bands. It's better known as the Möbius Strips. It's named after a German mathematician and astronomer, August Ferdinand Möbius, who discovered its properties. Now you can, too!

The Möbius Strips involve topology, which is the study of shapes that get distorted (stretched or shrunk). You can call it the study of elastic objects. More specifically, topology looks at what stays the same in an object when you distort it (by stretching or shrinking).

As a magic trick, this is sometimes performed with bands of cloth that are ripped in half, but it's also done with strips of paper that are cut along the center. It's easier to use paper.

First we'll learn how to make Möbius Strips and some of the basic effects you can create. Then we'll learn a fun magic routine you can perform with them.

🖝 Materials

Paper
Scotch® tape or paper glue
Scissors
Pen or pencil

Making Möbius Strips

Cut a strip of paper about 8 inches (20 cm) long and 2 inches (5 cm) wide. Or you can use calculator paper that you can get from office supply stores. Give the strip a half-twist (turn one side over) and tape or glue the two ends together. Ta-daa, you've just made a Möbius Strip!

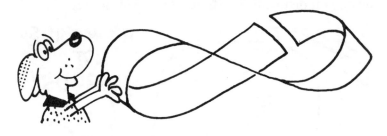

Möbius Fact 1: A Möbius Strip has only one side and only one edge. If you trace down the center of the strip (or along the edge) all the way around, you'll find that you've drawn one long loop.

Möbius Fact 2: Cut another strip of paper, and draw a line down the center of each side. Then give it a half-twist and tape or glue the ends together. Now cut the strip in half along the line you drew. Instead of getting two halves, you'll get one giant loop.

Möbius Fact 3: Cut another strip of paper. This time, draw a line on each side about a third of the way from the edge. Then twist and tape, or glue, as before. Cut the strip along the lines. You'll have to cut twice around. You'll end up with two loops linked together. If you cut the smaller loop in half along the center, you'll get another larger loop that's still linked to the other.

Möbius Fact 4: This time cut two strips of paper the same length. Lay one exactly on top of the other. Then, holding them together as if they're one strip, give them the half-twist. Tape or glue the top strip into a loop. Then tape or glue the bottom strip. The two strips should be nested together but not actually attached. If you put a pencil or your finger between the strips and trace all the way around, you can see that they're not attached. Now, if you gently pull the nested strips apart, you'll find you have one giant loop.

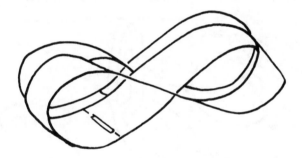

Möbius Fact 5: Make the nested strips as you did in Fact 4. Now cut along the center. You'll get two loops linked together.

You can find Möbius Strips at work for things other than magic. They are the fan belts in cars, and they are also used in some film and tape recorders. Since a Möbius Strip has only one side, it wears out very evenly and doesn't have to be replaced so often.

THE AFGHAN BANDS

Here's a classic magic routine that makes use of the Möbius Strip. It combines all of the facts you've just learned to tell a magical story.

☒ The Effect

You show a large loop of paper (or cloth) and cut (or rip) it lengthwise into two separate rings. You rip one of these in two and it becomes a single loop that's twice as big as the original. Then you rip the other loop in half and it produces two separate linked rings.

✍ Materials

Paper or a lightweight, cheap cotton cloth
Scissors
Scotch® tape or paper glue (for paper)
Needle and thread (for cloth)

☞ Preparation

Make a strip about 3 feet (1 m) long and about 8 inches (20 cm) wide.

At each end of the strip, cut a slit up the center about 4 inches (10 cm) long.

Take one part (above the slit) of one end, give it a half-twist (turn it over) and glue it to the same part at the other end. If you are using cloth, you could sew it together.

Take the other part of one end, give it a full twist (turn it over once, then again) and glue (or sew) it to the remaining part of the other end.

Finally, cut a slit lengthwise across the glued (or sewed) sections. These slits will give you a place to start cutting (or tearing) during the routine.

The Routine and Patter

NOTE: This is a classic story from the 1800s. You can make up your own story to tell while you're performing the trick.

1. Show the loop to the audience. It isn't absolutely necessary to hide the small twists and cuts from the audience, but it's probably better if they don't see them. The easiest way is to hold the loop so the twist and cuts face away from the audience.

2. Say, "Once there was a circus that had an emergency. Just before a big show, two of the performers lost their belts. In a panic, they asked the magician for help. 'I can fix that,' said the magician. She took off her belt and cut it in half."

3. Cut the loop in half lengthwise along the center (starting from the slit you made before) to produce two separate rings. (Remember: One of the rings will have a half-twist in it and the other will have a full twist.)

4. Say, "The first performer complained. 'That doesn't solve anything,' he said. 'I'm the giant. That belt will never fit me.' The magician said, 'No problem.' She cut one of the belts in half and it doubled in size!"

5. Cut the loop with the half-twist lengthwise along its center to produce the giant loop.

6. Say, "The other sideshow performer also complained. 'That's great for him, but what about us?' Sure enough, it was the ventriloquist and his dummy. 'No problem,' said the magician. She cut the other belt in half and magically saved the day."

7. Cut the other loop (the one with the full twist) lengthwise in half to produce the two separate, linked rings.

INSTA-LINK

Here's a fast and simple magic trick that also involves some topology. Remember that topology is a branch of mathematics that deals with stretching or twisting different kinds of shapes—more specifically, what stays the same when shapes are stretched or twisted.

🎩 The Effect
You attach two paper clips to a single bill of paper money. When you pull on the ends of the bill, the clips link together.

☞ Materials
Two paper clips
A bill of paper money or a piece of paper that's about the same size

The Routine
1. Fold the bill into a Z shape. You don't have to crease it. As long as the curves resemble a Z, that's fine.

2. Attach one paper clip to the first and second folds of the bill (from one end of the bill to the center section). Attach the other clip to the second and third folds of the bill (from the center section to the other end of the bill).

3. Quickly pull the two ends of the bill apart, straightening it out. The paper clips will link together and fall off the bill.

FLIP-FLOP GLASSES

This is a quick trick that you can puzzle people with at the dinner table. It makes use of the shape of drinking glasses and the fact that most people won't notice right away if rows of glasses are all mouth-up or mouth-down.

🎩 The Effect
Line up three glasses. Two are standing upright and one is mouth-down. In three moves, you set them all upright. No one else will be able to match your moves.

☜ Materials
Three empty drinking glasses

The Routine
1. Set up three glasses in a row. The center glass should be right-side up and the outer two should be mouth-side down.

2. Tell your audience that the object of this puzzle is to turn two glasses over at a time, and, in three moves, to have them all right-side up.

3. Let's call the glasses A, B, and C. At the beginning, A and C are mouth-down, and B is right-side up. Demonstrate your trick this way:

    a. Take glasses A and B, one in each hand, and turn them over.

    b. Do the same with glasses A and C.

    c. Do it once more with A and B.

4. All glasses should be right-side up. Now turn over glass B and ask someone to do what you just did. They will never be able to repeat your trick.

The Secret

When you started, glasses A and C were mouth-down and glass B was right-side up. After you demonstrated how to do it, you set them up so that glasses A and C are right-side up and glass B is mouth-down.

Most people won't notice this sneaky turnaround. In this new formation, there is no way to have them finish right-side up in three moves.

TANGLED COUPLE

Here's another trick involving the topology of knots and linkages. As in the trick "Insta-Link," you are changing the shape of something to create a magical-looking effect. Remember that topology deals with what stays the same when a shape is changed. In this trick, you "unlink" two lengths of string without having to cut or untie them.

The Effect

You tie your wrists together with a long piece of string. Your spectator does the same, but links their piece of string around yours. You both appear to be linked, but you are able to escape easily.

Materials

Two long pieces of string or rope, about 12–20 inches (30–50 cm) long

The Routine

IMPORTANT: Make sure that you tie the knots loosely, and that everything is comfortable.

1. Tie one end of the string around one wrist and the other end around the other wrist. There should be a length of string between your hands.

2. Have your spectator do the same, but before tying the second end of string link their piece of string around yours.

3. Ask if anyone can figure out how to get out of this puzzle without cutting or untying the string.

The Secret

The answer to this puzzle is simpler than it looks. Pass the center of one string under the string around the other person's wrist, then over that person's hand and back under their string.

*J*HRINKING COIN

Paper doesn't stretch, right? This trick will make you think again.

There is more topology at play in this trick. Here, you are actually changing the shape of a hole cut into a piece of paper.

🎩 The Effect

You show a piece of paper with a hole cut into it the size of a small coin. You ask if it's possible to push a larger coin through that hole without tearing the paper. To everyone's surprise, you are able to pass a quarter through the hole.

☜ Materials

    A small coin
    A larger coin
    Pencil
    Paper
    Scissors

☜ Preparation

You will need to experiment a bit with different coins. The circumference of the small coin (the length around the edge) needs to be a little bit more than twice the larger coin's diameter (the length across the center).

Place the smaller coin on a piece of paper and trace a line around its edge. Very carefully, cut along the line to make a hole the same size as the coin.

The Routine

1. Show the paper and demonstrate the exact size of the hole by fitting it over the smaller coin.

2. Show the size of the smaller coin in relation to the larger coin by placing one on top of the other. Ask if it's possible to pass the larger coin through the hole without tearing the paper.

The Secret

Fold the paper across the hole with the larger coin inside. The top of the coin should just fit through the hole.

You can now push the larger coin carefully through the hole. With the paper folded across the hole, it will actually widen enough to fit around the coin.

EDGE MAGIC

This is a visually startling trick that you can do at the dinner table. It makes use of the shape of forks—their length and their ability to wedge together on a coin.

♟ The Effect
With two forks and a coin, you demonstrate an amazing feat of balance.

☞ Materials
Two forks
A drinking glass
A large coin (The trick can also work with a smaller coin, but then you'll need to use smaller forks, such as dessert forks.)

The Routine

1. Turn the forks sideways and hold them so that they are facing you. Overlap the prongs of the two forks and insert the coin between the middle prongs of each fork. The coin should hold the two forks together loosely.

2. Place the edge of the coin on the edge of a drinking glass. The forks should curve toward the glass. With some practice, you will find the right position to make them balance on the edge of the glass.

The Secret

The trick works because the long handles of the forks curve towards the glass. This moves the center of gravity for the construction (coin and forks) to a point right underneath the spot where the coin rests on the glass. This puts the forks and coin in a state of stable equilibrium.

INDEX